Cataloging-in-Publication Data is available from the Library of Congress.

ISBN: 9781520663029
10 09 08 07 06 5 4 3 2

Published by
Southeast Research
An African American Experience Project

Horace King

From Slave, to Master Builder and Legislator

J. David Dameron

Southeast Research
An African American Experience Project

For the Honorable George R. Greene (1950-2014), in memoriam. Historian, Jurist and my good friend.

J. David Dameron

Contents

Preface

Let's discuss this book for a moment before getting into the story (the purpose of a preface section in a book). This book also has some things you may not yet be familiar with but they are very easy to learn.

For example, each photograph and map in this book has a description underneath it that describes where it came from (and where you could go to learn more about it).

There are also numbers at the end of some paragraphs that mean to look near the back of the book in the End Notes (Sources) section where you can learn where the information came from and where you can learn more about it.

I believe that young readers want to learn more than teachers have time to provide in the classroom (they're very busy teaching us). So, I have included several reference tools for you to learn about and explore (make it interactive by using them, I think you'll enjoy it).

Also, someday when you're in a class and your teacher shows you how to use these tools, you'll already know about them. You can then share this knowledge with your friends and they'll be impressed-Not.

Seriously though, this book is written for teens and young readers to enjoy, and it is written in such a way to maximize enjoyment but also to transfer knowledge about a "great American" who lived a long time ago and how non-fiction (true) history books are arranged and presented in the higher college level books. You might as well learn now because it's quite simple.

As you certainly know by now, there is a lot of history for students to learn. From World to United States history and on down to local histories, there is a vast amount of information to study, and no one person knows it all.

And, while our education systems are masters at providing students an overview of the highlights of history, there simply is not enough time in the classroom to learn many of the fascinating, real-life stories of people hidden just beneath the common curriculum level. After all, what is not history?

In fact, everything that has happened in the past to include every single human being on the planet creates our history. Accordingly, each person creates his or her own history and you share it with the people around you, which creates our collective histories and the true stories (or history) of our society. It was the same for the folks who lived before us and so our teachers are very busy assisting young people by guiding their studies of history.

It would be genuinely sad if an American student didn't know about George Washington and George Washington Carver (let's call them the "Two Georges," okay?) for that matter. So, curriculums focus on the key people and events to learn in history classes, otherwise, we would all be stuck in High School for ever.

However, teens and young readers alike can also study all they want on their own time and therein lies the wondrous world that history provides us all. The folks that went before us fought and earned our freedom so let's show some respect and read all we want to on our own time, okay?

Have you ever wondered if someday, people may study about you and your experiences? It's a reality to consider. Do you think when the "Two Georges" were young that they ever imagined young students would someday study about them?

So, let's consider the relevance of Horace King. In this book, you will learn that he was born a slave but he won his freedom, worked real hard and achieved great things.

As you read through this book keep in mind that slaves had no rights. They were bound by law as servants to their masters and they had to do as they were told.

We all know that slavery is wrong but remember as you read, in the timeframe this book covers (1807-1885), life was very different from our world today.

So, enjoy your reading and I think you'll find the true story of Horace King to be very interesting.

Acknowledgments

I must begin by telling you about a man who was my good friend, George Greene because it was he who taught me about Horace King.

George was born and raised in the Chattahoochee Valley of Georgia and Alabama. The mighty river that flows through this fertile valley also serves as a boundary between the states of Alabama and Georgia. So, after high school, George went to Auburn University and the University of Alabama where he received academic degrees in History and Law (he was wicked smart)!

In fact, with his law degree, George was a very well respected lawyer and he was a judge in Russell County, Alabama. He was one of the longest serving judges in the State of Alabama history. With 34 years of public service as a judge, which is certainly a very long time and a lot of hard work serving his community (which he loved very much).

George participated in a lot of civic and state public service organizations including the establishment of the "Cora Reid Greene Home for Children." This wonderful foster home for children was established in honor of George's mother, Mrs. Cora Greene.

In his spare time, George established the Greene Museum, which focuses on the history of the Chattahoochee Valley. George built a great collection of historical artifacts and documents (archives), which he used to introduce the wonders of their local history to a lot of people. He adored young people and they very much enjoyed his museum (really cool stuff) and they especially loved to hear him tell stories of long ago.

What always impressed me about George was his recollection of facts as his brain worked like a computer in recalling dates, names and events. George also collected old letters, photographs and rare antique books written long ago.

But the greatest gift George afforded me was his time and friendship. He loved to talk about people that had lived a long time ago in the area as if they were still around. He had learned a lot of local history just by talking to the families of those people and he knew a lot about them as well as the local history.

The archives of George Greene were compiled from decades of his own personal research. George freely provided me with many of the photos and historical information in this book about Horace King. George and I conducted several historical projects together and it was an honor and privilege to know him.

In fact, George and I worked on material for a book on Horace King and another African American known as "Blind Tom." Unfortunately, George suffered from several illnesses and he died before we could complete the project. So, I dedicate this book to the memory of Judge George Greene. Someday, I'll try to complete George's story of "Blind Tom" for publication as well.

Do a Google search on "Blind Tom" Wiggins. He was an amazing musician. Although he was blind and autistic, he was a brilliant pianist.

I also owe a great deal of gratitude to several other people and local institutions of learning who helped me as well. Dr. John Lupold and Dr. Craig Lloyd, archivists and historians at Columbus State University provided numerous details about Horace King and the local area (they have a great archival collection and library).

In fact, Dr. Lupold along with Thomas French authored an extensive book about Horace King entitled *Bridging Deep South Rivers: The Life and Legend of Horace King.* Published in 2004 by the University of Georgia Press, this book provides the definitive and detailed study of Horace King for adult readers. Someday, if you would like to more about Horace King, read their book (it's filled with details).

Ms. Kaye Minchew, the Director of the Troup County Archives was very helpful and guided me to key holdings regarding Horace King in their archives. The ladies at the Chattahoochee Valley Community College were very helpful in providing information about the history of Phenix City and I thank them as well.

In the Columbus, Georgia area there is a vast treasure of real historical artifacts and archive collections in several awesome museums. I am most grateful to the Columbus Museum and make sure you visit there if you get the chance. Their museum has the original photographs of Horace and Frances King along with many other very cool items (check it out)!

I also thank: the National Civil War Naval Museum; the National Infantry Museum (in Columbus, Georgia); the Troup County Archives (LaGrange, Georgia); Muscogee County Archives (Columbus, Georgia); the Russell County Archives (Phenix City, Alabama); the Alabama Department of Archives & History (Montgomery, Alabama); the Georgia Department of Archives & History (Morrow, Georgia), the National Archives and the Library of Congress (both in Washington D.C.). Their staffs are very helpful, friendly and they provided me with a wealth of material for this book.

I highly encourage anyone who has an opportunity to visit these museums. Your visit would be time well spent, and a lot of fun. You will also find the people that work in them to be very helpful in helping with research and exploring our past.

Chapter 1

While Horace King is certainly less familiar in American History than men such as George Washington or George Washington Carver, it does not mean he was unimportant or less worth reading about. In the words of his peers, Horace King was simply a good man and a highly skilled carpenter. He was also described as a determined man, highly confident, very intelligent and extremely trustworthy.

A builder by trade as well as by deeds, Horace King spent his life constructing foundations, pillars, and bridging gaps throughout his community. While other men have certainly achieved a fine reputation as a good person, several things about Horace King make him a little different.

Horace King began his life as a slave and was bound to a life filled with hard labor and adversity. His story reflects the inherent strength of determination and the power of the human spirit. Despite bondage, racial prejudice and a multitude of obstacles, King focused his life on building things and being a genuinely good man.

Throughout his life's work, King employed the virtues of honesty and respect for his fellow man. Ultimately, dignity, respect and freedom were his rewards, as he transcended the color lines inherent in the Old South of the nineteenth century. Today, Horace King's legacy is as powerfully symbolic as one of his sturdy bridges.

One may ask, how many people in American History began their life as a slave yet won their freedom and became a respected community leader? The answer of course is very few and Mr. King stands above most of these people as a shining example of the virtues of determination, goodness and hard work.

Horace King rose from a life of adversity and became affectionately known as Horace "The Bridge Builder" King and the "Prince of Bridge Builders." He also served his community in many important civic capacities including that of State Legislator. How is it possible that this man achieved so much although he was born a slave?

Slave labor on a plantation in the "Old South"
Harpers Weekly, July 29, 1865

Chapter 2

Horace King was born on September 8, 1807, in Cheraw, South Carolina. His father was Edmund King, a Negro slave, and his mother was Susan King, a Catawba Indian, both of whom were the property of a local physician named King and the source of the family's surname. Upon his father's death, Horace was sold as property first to Mr. Jennings Dunlop (a slave trader) and then to his final owner, Mr. John Godwin, a builder. (1)

As a young man, Horace was educated to read and write at a time when educating blacks was viewed as unnecessary and in some places, it was even a crime. However, his new owner was a genteel man and he and Horace began a lifelong friendship that spanned many decades. Mr. Godwin decided that Horace would make a fine carpenter and so he educated him and put him to work.

John Godwin was a master builder and Mason. As Horace matured, he served his master as a construction laborer while absorbing his new skills and he excelled at everything he did. Horace adopted a saying that he often repeated to himself and others, "ignorance breeds poverty."

As an adult, Horace King gained his master's confidence as a trustworthy and energetic supervisor of his fellow slaves and together, in 1827, Godwin and King built a covered bridge that spanned the Pee Dee River in Cheraw, South Carolina.

Pee Dee River Covered Bridge (1ˢᵗ Godwin/ King bridge). George Greene Collection

This was a very important project for both Godwin and King as this bridge was one of the first "Town Lattice Truss" covered bridges to be built outside of New England. This type of covered bridge was designed and patented in 1820 by Ithiel Town, an inventor and builder from Connecticut. (2)

Over time, King began to master bridge building and Godwin entrusted King to supervisory duties and relied on him more and more. King's abilities as a bridge builder and more importantly his ability to lead others provided him a dignified position and respected authority.

Red Oak Bridge constructed by Horace King and sons using the "Town Lattice" design.
Author's Collection

Town's patented design employs the use of "treenails" (pronounced trunnels), or large wooden pegs that are hammered into drilled holes to connect the bridge's timbers. Using a lattice design framework, diagonal planks form a sturdy interwoven (criss-crossed) truss system at 45 to 60 degree angles. The trusses are firmly anchored together with treenails and length-wise chords along the top and bottom of the latticework.

This bridging system was not only efficient, but also economical. More importantly, bridge construction would forge a solid reputation and provide a livelihood for both Godwin and King for the rest of their lives.

In October of 1832, Mr. Godwin moved his family and slaves west into Georgia as the former Creek Indian territories were opened to settlement. Godwin chose the bustling town of Columbus, Georgia as their new home.

Columbus was a newly established trading town located in the heart of Georgia, and along its western border with the state of Alabama. The City of Columbus is laid out along the eastern shore of the Chattahoochee River, which is a prime location as a regional agricultural, shipping, and industrial center.

In this location, Godwin's construction business enjoyed bountiful opportunities and he capitalized on the region's needs by building homes and developing commercial properties.

Shortly after arriving in Columbus, the City Council solicited the community for bids to build a bridge across the Chattahoochee River. The bridge was needed to join the Georgia community with its neighbors on the opposite shore in Alabama.

Across the river in Alabama lay the quaint little town of Girard (now Phenix City), Alabama, and a ferry simply could not meet the requirements of the ever-expanding community as both towns lay on the Federal Road. This major artery of transportation brought settlers from the east into the newly forming states and ever-expanding western territories.

Godwin won the bid for the proposed bridge, and the city awarded him a $14,000 contract to construct it. He then placed an advertisement in the local paper for additional laborers, and soon the massive project was underway.

Godwin engaged Horace King to supervise the small army of local carpenters that felled trees, milled lumber, and managed all the myriad tasks required to span the Chattahoochee River using a sturdy covered "Town Lattice Truss" bridge. The Chattahoochee River is powerful and prone to flooding. Additionally, the bridge had to support a great number of travelers, horses, mules, wagons and carriages. (3)

Completed in 1833, this bridge spanned the 400+ feet between the shores of the Chattahoochee River and it was originally known as "City Bridge," but its name was later changed to the Dillingham Street Bridge.

Hailed as one of the finest bridges in the south, the City Bridge soon had Godwin and King busy with numerous requests to build their Town Lattice Truss bridges throughout the region. Ultimately, all the bridges that were built across the Chattahoochee River (north and south) of Columbus were built by Godwin and King.

During the next few years, Godwin also contracted to build bridges in Tallassee and Tuscaloosa, Alabama. Horace King mastered the art of bridge building by experience and hard work.

In 1838, Godwin and King accepted the challenge of spanning the Chattahoochee below Columbus at Irwinton (now Eufaula, Alabama).

This bridge exceeded 800 feet in length and lasted for many years despite tremendous floods and the continuous pressures of a mighty river.

While Godwin achieved great success with his bridges, he paid a fortune in royalty fees for many years to the lattice bride designer, Ithiel Town (due to patent rights) at the rate of $1.00 per linear foot.

Bridge completed in 1839 by Horace King over the Chattahoochee River at Eufaula, Alabama.

George Greene Collection

Godwin's reputation for construction excellence and skilled craftsmanship won him lucrative contracts in and around Columbus. More and more, Godwin relied upon his trusted slave, Horace King to supervise massive projects, and the two men forged unique bonds at a time when blacks and whites simply did not mix openly in society. Nonetheless, the two men were simply good friends and proud of their relationship.

King's reputation as an independent man of intelligence and skill won him the title of "The Prince of Bridge Builders," and "Horace, the Bridge Builder King." (4)

In 1839, Godwin and King built another expanse across the Chattahoochee, north of Columbus at West Point, Georgia. This was a very important event for Horace King as the building of this bridge was accomplished in the same year that his master granted him permission for marriage. Horace chose a beautiful young local girl of Indian descent to be his bride. On April 28, 1839 Horace and Frances King were married and they quickly started a family.

Chapter 3

During the next several years Horace worked hard managing construction projects, and he and his young bride also built their family. Ultimately, Horace and Frances were blessed with five children: Washington, Marshall, John, Annie Elizabeth, and George.

As explained by Horace's granddaughter, Theodora Thomas, "Washington was named for Horace's brother, Marshall was named for the Indian Chief in Phenix City, Alabama, and John was named for his friend (and master) John Godwin." (5)

Mr. and Mrs. Horace King
Courtesy of Columbus (Georgia) Museum

Between the years 1839 and 1846, Godwin and King built numerous bridges and several large commercial building projects. Amongst their construction achievements during this time are the: Muscogee County (Georgia) Courthouse; Russell County (Alabama) Courthouse; Bryant (13th Street Bridge) in Columbus, Georgia; Red Oak Creek Bridge in Woodbury, Georgia (Meriwether County, and still standing); Wetumpka Bridge in Elmore County, Alabama; and several other smaller bridges in Florence and Lafayette, Alabama. (6)

Godwin had a very large home constructed for his family on 14th Street in Girard, Alabama and on an adjoining property, Godwin provided King with a modest home as well (King Street in that same town is also named for Horace).

The town of Girard, Alabama (known today as Phenix City) was a bustling little town filled with construction projects. With the larger town of Columbus, Georgia just across the Chattahoochee River, the services of Godwin and King were in great demand for their construction skills.

Warehouses, mills, bridges, churches, homes, and business offices were planned and built by Godwin and King not only in Girard and Columbus, but throughout the Chattahoochee Valley region.

The area grew rapidly and by 1861, the Chattahoochee Valley region was providing manufactured goods throughout the south and shipping cotton down the river to the Gulf of Mexico, where it was loaded on larger steamships bound for England and other European ports.

Dillingham Street (aka City Bridge), Columbus, Georgia.
George Greene Collection

*Dillingham Street (aka City) Bridge,
Columbus, Georgia (opposing angle).
George Greene Collection*

A special bond had been forged between Godwin and King and despite their social difference and a master-slave arrangement, the two men and their families grew ever closer.

Yet, while the construction projects provided Godwin with success, in 1846 his health began a long and continuous downfall, which simultaneously affected his finances.

Despite numerous lucrative offers, Godwin refused to sell his slave and close friend, Horace King. Reverend Francis Cherry, a local man who personally knew Horace King recorded that:

> Horace, though a man of superior capacity and intelligence, and was respected as such by all classes, never lost sight of his social position by intruding himself beyond his legitimate sphere, which exalted rather than diminished him in public esteem.
> His apt capacity for business and his unimpeachable trustworthiness naturally excited the cupidity of speculators, and as high as $6000 was offered for him. But it appears that a mutual attachment and confidence had sprung up between him and his old master and family who was in no humor to trade, consequently no money could buy him. (7)

[No. 292.] AN ACT

To emancipate Horace King, a slave.

Whereas, it appears by the petition of John Godwin, Ann H. Godwin, and William C. Wright, that it is their intention to emancipate and set free Horace King of Russell county: Therefore,

Section 1. *Be it enacted by the Senate and House of Representatives of the State of Alabama, in General Assembly convened,* That the said Horace King is hereby declared to be free, and his emancipation is hereby confirmed, and the said Horace King shall not be required to leave the State of Alabama, upon the condition that the said John Godwin, Ann H. Godwin and William C. Wright, or any one of them, shall enter into bond with approved security, to the Judge of the County Court of Russell, in the sum of one thousand dollars; conditioned that the said Horace King shall never become a charge to this State, or any county or town therein.

Approved, 3d February, 1846.

State of Alabama Emancipation of Horace King (1846).
George Greene Collection

17

In recognition of his friendship for King and to ensure his freedom, Godwin successfully petitioned the Alabama General Assembly and on February 3, 1846, Act Number 292 states that Horace King "is declared to be free." (8)

Assisting Godwin in this matter was an influential Alabama politician named Robert Jemison Jr. whose friendship was of great value to both Godwin and King. Jemison served in the Alabama state legislature, 1837-63, and during the Civil War he served in the Confederate Congress, 1863-65.

Robert Jemison Jr.
George Greene Collection

As Godwin's health declined, Horace King assumed all the duties of his former owner to include caring for both of their families. As stated by Reverend Cherry, "This change in relations in life made no change in Horace King's sense of obligation to his former master."

In fact, Horace had been treated by Godwin for many years with the same confidence and liberty as though he had been a free man. Horace King "never abused it, and now that he was legally a free man, his master continued to stand first and foremost in his respect and calculations for the future." (9)

Mutual respect and a successful business venture forged powerful bonds of friendship between these two men. Horace King and John Godwin were genuinely close friends and their former master-slave relationship did not stand in their way.

Chapter 4

During the 1850s, King supervised the construction of several bridges. Chief amongst these endeavors was the railroad bridge across the Chattahoochee River joining by rail the city of Columbus, Georgia with its neighbor, Girard, Alabama in 1855.

This important bridge and railroad ensured that bulk industrial and agricultural products passed freely through Columbus eastward to Savannah, Georgia and westward to Montgomery, Alabama.

Advertisement placard for labor on the Mobile and Girard Railroad (The slave masters got the money unless the Negroes were freedmen).
George Greene Collection

In 1858, King also supervised the construction of a major bridge across the Flint River in Albany, Georgia. In addition to the bridge projects, King also constructed several homes, and commercial projects that included an elegant free-standing spiral staircase in the capitol building in Montgomery. (10)

By 1859, John Godwin's investment schemes and railroad ventures such as the Mobile and Girard RR line failed. Godwin financially lost all his holdings and his health rapidly failed him as well. On February 26, 1859, he died.

Godwin's dear friend and former slave, Horace King took care of all of the arrangements including an expensive and beautiful marble obelisk, which states, "This stone was placed here by Horace King. In lasting remembrance of the love and gratitude he felt for his lost friend and former master."

Many years later, Robert Ripley wrote about King's admiration of his former master in his "Ripley's Believe It or Not," news article. "While their friendship may have seemed odd (due to race relations back then) to some people, clearly their life-long bonds are perpetually declared on that monument."

King continued looking after Godwin's family for many years and he even moved out of his own home to provide a house for the family of Godwin's daughter. King also had his own family to support and he managed to send his son Marshall to college in Oberlin, Ohio.

During this time, Horace King visited his son in Ohio and while he was there, in the words of King's friend, Reverend Francis Cherry, King was "initiated into the sublime mysteries of the ancient order of Free and Accepted Masons, in the State of Ohio, the laws of the craft not permitting it in Alabama at the time. And it is known that he was accepted, respected, recognized and honored as a Mason in good standing all his life." (11)

John Godwin had been a member of the Freemasons as were many other prominent members of society and King's affiliation with this organization was a valuable accomplishment as it secured many fraternal connections across the racial boundaries of that era.

As the nation ushered in the 1860s along with the American Civil War, the Columbus area became a mighty industrial center that was second only to Richmond, Virginia in its war production capabilities. When the Civil War began in 1861, Free Negroes in the southern states had to make serious choices regarding their livelihood.

King decided to remain in the south and continue his construction business. Even though he was a free man, he supported his friends (black and white) and he reluctantly chose to be a citizen of the newly formed Confederate States of America (CSA).

King was a well-respected man, and despite his heritage, whites treated him in a manner appropriate to the prevailing norms associated with a free man of color. After all, his family, friends, and business interests were so entrenched in the community; to move northward was simply not a viable option. Several African Americans even fought alongside their white masters and long-time family friends in the war.

Many of King's friends served in the Confederacy. John Godwin's sons, who were the same age as King's sons served in the Confederate military. Captain John D. Godwin served in the 28th Battalion Georgia Siege Artillery and Private Thomas M. Godwin served in the 34th Alabama Infantry. While John D. survived the war, Thomas died during the Chattanooga Campaign in December of 1863. (12)

Confederate Soldiers (A.M. Chandler and Silas Chandler, LC-DIG-ppmsca-40073), Library of Congress Prints and Photographs Division

Chapter 5

The realities of war hit the region hard. For the first few years of the war the King family continued their lives with few negative consequences other than tremendous pressures to make a choice between serving either the USA or the CSA.

King simply wanted to enjoy the solitude and freedom he so rightly deserved. While he considered himself to be a Union man, he loved the south, and the local community in which he lived.

As time and the war marched on, attrition of men and resources led to suffering and the southern economy spiraled downward and out of control. Simultaneously, the Union pressed southward in 1864 and the Confederate government was forced into drastic measures to thwart immediate disaster.

In 1863, the Confederate authorities pressured its citizens to give their all for the war. While the Confederacy was eagerly supported throughout the southern states, the people of the Chattahoochee Valley gave not only their sons, but also clothing, food, and resources on a scale that exceeded the norm.

Even the church bells and family brass were collected and smelted into cannons in the local factories. When Atlanta was threatened with Union invasion, the hospitals were relocated to Columbus, Georgia where the local ladies provided their own meager food stores and provided care for the beleaguered troops.

1863 Confederate Navy receipt for Horace King contract work.
George Greene Collection

Columbus also housed a Naval Port facility on the Chattahoochee River where boats were constructed for the Confederacy. With the local ironworks and other facilities available, Port Columbus provided a strategic location with which to safely build and launch ironclad vessels southward into the Gulf of Mexico. This facility and the Confederate Navy is where King found the security he desperately sought for his family.

In May of 1863, Horace King began working for the Confederate Navy as a contracted employee. King was provided with an excellent salary and his work included the supervision of felling trees, planing (trimming and shaping) timbers, making "tree nails", and general carpentry work in support of constructing Confederate ironclad war ships such as the C.S.S. Jackson (aka CSS Muskogee) and the C.S.S. Chattahoochee.

C.S.S. Jackson (1864), USN Catalog #: NH 48026, United States Department of the Navy, US Naval Historical Center.

C.S.S. Jackson (1964), USN Catalog #: NH 45769, Georgia Historical Commission. U.S. Naval History and Heritage Command Photograph. Note: Although burned to the waterline and years later retrieved from the Chattahoochee River, the condition of the timbers is still solid. The ship's hull is on exhibit at the Confederate Naval Museum, Columbus, Georgia.

King also received substantial compensation for the use of his wagons, additional required laborers, and the products these men made. King also received a salary at the rate of $87.50 for a two-week period while the Chief Naval Foreman earned a salary of $150.00 for the same time. In contrast, the average common laborer working for these men earned $3.00 per day. (13)

Thus, King gained respect in his community as he provided a valuable service to the nation (CSA) in which he lived. Moreover, he and his family also remained unmolested by anyone who may have doubted their loyalty at a time when pro-Unionists were being accused of plotting subversion against the Confederacy.

Early in 1864, a desperate Confederate administration passed a conscript bill that sought to force free men of color into the armed forces. Faced with the near certainty of his sons being conscripted into the Confederate Army, King wrote an anxious letter to his friend, Robert Jemison Jr. seeking information and advice concerning his dilemma.

Per the conscript bill all free men of color, aged 18-50 were to be inducted immediately into the Confederate Army. In his urgent letter to Jemison, dated March 23, 1864, King stated that he was opposed to his sons going to war, and more importantly, these young adults had no desire to serve in uniform.

King also declared, "Myself and the children have been working for the government for over a year and I would like to know where we stand if we should not continue to work for the government, and I want to know where we stand if we stop." (14)

Robert Jemison had invested heavily in bridges constructed by Horace King and he genuinely treated Horace as a close friend. Housed in the University of Alabama Archives are the only surviving letters between Jemison and Jemison. Apparently, Jemison genuinely believed in Horace's skills and he often took his advice. Jemison even stated that Horace King was the most honest man he knew, black or white.

While Horace King was fifty-seven years old and well beyond conscript age, and his youngest son, George was only fourteen and not yet eligible for military service, his other sons faced certain conscription as Washington was 21, Marshall was 20, and John was 18 years old.

Despite King's efforts to avoid the inevitable, his sons were soon notified to report to the Confederate authorities. King immediately appealed to his supervisor Samuel Whitesides at the Naval base.

King secured an arrangement wherein his sons could work for their father and assist in construction of the war ships and other projects as required by the Confederate Navy.

For the next several months, King and his sons worked diligently for the Navy, but all too soon, they were relocated to Carroll County, Georgia where they were required built a railroad bridge for the (CSA) Mobile and Florence line. They were also forced to build river obstructions to defend against Union gunboat incursions, and reluctantly they did comply with their orders.

While King's wife and daughter moved temporarily to live within the vicinity of the construction project, the family was restricted from frequent visits. Nonetheless, the family pushed through and survived the ordeal by doing hard work and following the restrictions and travels imposed upon them.

King's wife had rented a farm nearby the work project at Moore's Bridge, which Horace had built years earlier for Mr. James D. Moore of Carroll County. Mrs. King acted as the local bridge toll collector for Mr. Moore until a Union cavalry raid led by General George Stoneman in July of 1864 destroyed the bridge much to the Kings' lament.

Sadly, Horace had accepted payment of forty shares of stock in the bridge in lieu of cash. Additionally, the Union raiders also took from the King family 7 mules, 1 horse, 1 wagon, 27,000 board feet of lumber, 400 pounds of bacon, 1,500 pounds of flour, 100 bushels of corn, and 200 pounds of sugar.

Thus, the King family suffered losses inflicted from both the Union and Confederacy during the Civil War. Years after the conflict, the King family filed claims against the federal government for their losses, but these claims were ultimately denied. (15)

On October 1, 1864, Horace received an even harsher blow than his losses incurred during the Stoneman Raid (Moore's Bridge, his food stores, and his construction resources were destroyed by the Union Army). Tragically, due to stress and illness, Frances L. King, his wife of twenty-four years died.

The loss of his dear wife was a great burden on Horace and the family (there were still three young teenagers at home) but they pushed on without her. Horace buried Frances in the local cemetery alongside the Godwin family in Girard, Alabama.

As if these setbacks were not enough for the beleaguered family, on April 16, 1865, in the final desperate days of the Civil War, Union General James Wilson and his Cavalry Corps raided the Chattahoochee Valley destroying everything in their path.

Wilson's initial targets of this raid were the strategic bridges that spanned the Chattahoochee River at Columbus and West Point, Georgia. In total, there were five bridges that crossed the region between the target areas, and Horace King had built them all.

Approaching from Alabama, the Union cavalry needed to get its massive army across the river to invade Georgia, and taking at least one bridge would save valuable time and resources for the Union invaders.

In simultaneous assaults, the Union forces successfully took the bridges, but the City Bridge (Dillingham Street Bridge) in Columbus, which was built by Horace King, was destroyed by fire during the battle. (16)

As the Union Army passed through the Chattahoochee region, they again confiscated horses, mules, and other valuable resources.

In an incident that reflects the importance of King's Masonic affiliation, a Union patrol again confiscated King's mules, but this time, Horace managed to persuade the commanding officer, who was also a Mason, that the army could do without his mules.

The officer complied with King's request and maintaining ownership of these highly needed (and valuable) resources was a great success for Horace King, and more importantly, it marked a turn of events for himself, his family, and his nation.

During the war, horses and mules were highly valued for pulling wagons, and hauling men and equipment. For Horace King, he could not continue his trade as the timbers used in construction were too large and heavy for men to move.

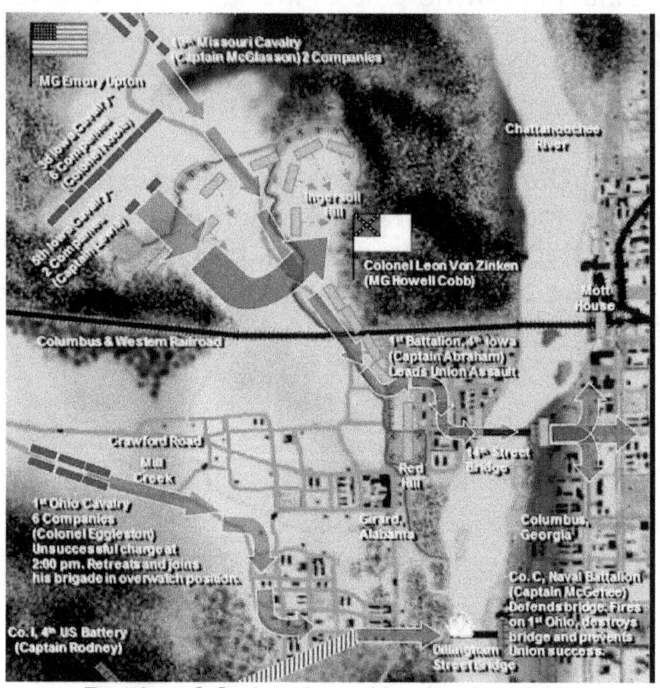

Battle of Columbus (April 16, 1865)
Author's Collection

In King's own words as described at the end of the war, "I was a colored man and was as much a Union man from beginning to the end as I dared to be. I felt glad that the thing [war] was done and was glad that the Union was restored." (17)

Chapter 6

With the war ended, reconstruction in the Chattahoochee Valley involved Horace King in many ways. With bridges to rebuild and a rejuvenated economy, Horace King engaged in more construction work than ever before.

Columbus, Georgia served as the King' primary construction efforts in the immediate post-war era. In 1865, Horace and his sons built a four-story textile mill known as Clapp's Factory, and in 1869 they rebuilt City Mills. In 1870 the King family construction business completed a railroad bridge for the Mobile and Girard Railroad.

19th Century lithograph of Columbus, Georgia (excerpt depicting several King construction projects-mill, bridges and houses). George Greene Collection

After the Civil War, the King family continued living in Girard (now Phenix City) in Russell County, Alabama. The Kings resided in a modest home just across the Chattahoochee River from Columbus, Georgia.

Horace was well known and liked throughout the community and he became active during the Reconstruction Era as a Registrar of voters. In 1868, King's friends urged him to run for political office, but he had no desire to enter politics.

African Americans voting for the first time during Reconstruction
Library of Congress, Prints and Photographs Division

Nonetheless, reluctantly, Horace King placed his name on the ballot and his popularity amongst blacks and whites alike was validated with a victory.

In 1868, King assumed his chair in the Alabama State Congress, but would not take up his new duties until completing an ongoing construction project, thus missing his first term in the legislature.

With political affairs then occupying his time, Horace gave more of the responsibilities of the construction business to his sons and he also took a new wife.

In 1869, at the age of 62, Horace King married Ms. Sally Jane McManus who was 27 years old. Horace King was reelected to a second term in the Alabama legislature, thus serving with distinction until finally stepping down in 1872.

Alabama Reconstruction Legislature in front of the State House (1872).
George Greene Collection

While serving in the Alabama House of Representatives, several southern communities and states passed laws that disenfranchised people of color by enacting "Black Codes." These measures were designed to create obstacles to the freedoms of blacks. One such code used literacy tests to determine if blacks were intelligent enough to vote.

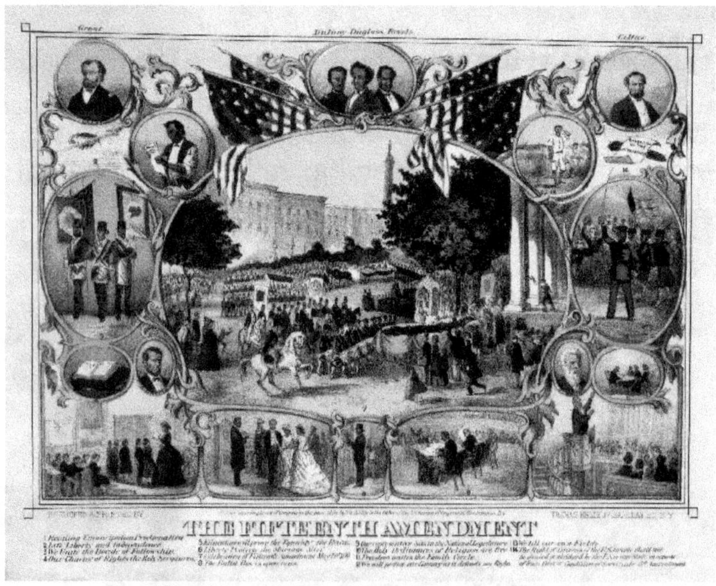

Ratified in 1870, the 15th Amendment of the US Constitution states, "The right of citizens...to vote shall not be denied or abridged...on account of race, color, or previous condition of servitude."
Library of Congress,
Prints and Photographs Division

The Alabama Reconstruction legislature worked hard to keep the "Black Codes" away from the polling booths and to maintain the security of freedom for all. Still, the US Congress had to enact the 15th Amendment to protect every race and secure their right to vote through a federal law that states cannot ignore.

As a legislator, Horace King introduced several bills, and one of these provided relief for laborers and mechanics. Another bill introduced by King required that convicts be forced to work on the public highways (chain gang).

King also served locally as the magistrate for Russell County, Alabama and he served as the registrar in his hometown of Girard and as a census compiler. In 1872, Horace King, his wife, and their sons and daughter, all relocated to LaGrange, Georgia. (18)

In LaGrange, the King family found a smaller, but quieter town and there was also plenty of work in the region. King's sons assumed the primary responsibilities of bridge building and they formed a formal partnership under the business name of the "King Brothers Bridge Company." King's daughter Annie was also employed at the firm.

The family prospered and built many of the homes in LaGrange including their own. Horace King was blessed with grandchildren and they all lived within walking distance of his home.

Horace King and sons (circa 1869).
Photos from W.H. Crogman's book entitled,
Progress of a Race.
George Greene Collection

The family business achieved numerous contracts and they built parts of LaGrange College and the Southern Female College, the Warren Street Methodist Church, the LaGrange Academy, and the Lee County Courthouse in Opelika, Alabama.

On October 5, 1883, a local paper, the _Opelika Times_ published an interview with Horace King conducted by his friend, Reverend Francis Cherry. Despite attaining a ripe old age, the interviewer describes Horace with:

> Horace King is now in his 77th year, and is full of wonderful vigor for his years. He is a little above medium size and height, with a complexion showing more his Indian blood that any other. His countenance is broad and open, eyes keen and black, his forehead indicative more of sound, practical, common sense, than brilliant talent. His hair is nearly straight and almost as white as snow, and he wears a small tuft of gray beard under his lower lip. His voice is soft and pleasant, and in conversation seldom rises above an ordinary tone. He is never demonstrative, and is choice in the selection of words without appearing to be so. (20)

But as always, the Kings were masters of bridge building and Horace King certainly derived pride from his sons' achievements. In fact, the Glass Bridge in West Point, Georgia was considered one of the finest and largest bridges in the south until 1954, when it was no longer needed. The construction of this huge bridge reemphasized that Horace King was still the "Prince of Bridge Builders." (19)

Horace King in his final years.
George Greene Collection

Horace's second wife passed before him and she was laid to rest in Phenix City, Alabama alongside his first love. Horace also outlived his son Marshall (1844-1879). Marshall was buried in a new family plot in the LaGrange Cemetery (adjacent to the Confederate section).

On May 27, 1885, the master bridge builder died in his home and Horace was buried beside his son. His obituary in the local paper states that King had "risen to prominence by force of genius and character... we trust that the grace of God bridged for him 'the narrow stream of death' and that he now rests from all earthly cares and labors in the peaceful land beyond the flood." (21)

King's surviving children, Washington (1843-1910), John (1846-1926), Annie Elizabeth (1848-1919), and George (1850-1899) followed in their Father's footsteps and built many bridges throughout the South.

While Horace King was revered in his local community, he outlived most of his influential friends and upon his death, his public memory quickly faded from the forefront of society.

Thus, King's public service record and his engineering achievements quietly slipped into the pages of history. While the local papers occasionally honored his deeds, those who knew him certainly felt his loss.

His funeral train passed through the LaGrange town square where blacks and whites alike paid their respects and wept as the community had suffered a great loss. His grave was not marked until several years later. Today, Horace King's grave is marked with a simple granite slab that states, *"Horace King, born September 8, 1807, died May 27, 1887 (incorrect date), Master Covered Bridge Builder."*

Bearing testament to this man's achievements are several bridges that remain in working order today. While several of King's bridges have been restored by the Georgia Department of Transportation as historic preservation projects, and one has been moved to Callaway Gardens as an ornamental property, the Red Oak Creek Bridge is still in service. Built by Horace King and his crew in 1840, "at 341 feet, including the approaches, this structure is the oldest and longest wooden covered bridge in Georgia." (22)

Red Oak Creek Bridge built by Horace King
(Meriwether County, Georgia).
Author's Collection

Located in Meriwether County, Georgia the local community still uses this bridge as if it were just any other modern roadway bridge. While the approach is well off the beaten path, it is located four miles north of Woodbury, Georgia, just off Highway 74 on Huel Brown Road (Covered Bridge Road).

It is truly amazing that this bridge has remained in service for nearly two-hundred years. Not only is this unique covered bridge sturdy, it's also elegant and reminds drivers of a by-gone day.

The new concrete Dillingham Street (aka City) Bridge, Columbus, Georgia occasionally gets flooded but the old bridge is honored there by a marker that was placed on the National Register in 1973 (marker is located on the southwest bank).

Overall, Horace King and his sons built at least 125 bridges. Twenty-five of these bridges are covered "Town Lattice" bridges with a length that exceeds 500 feet. The King bridges were built across every major river in Georgia, Alabama, eastern Mississippi, and the sole structure across the Pee Dee River in South Carolina, where the King bridge building legacy began. (23)

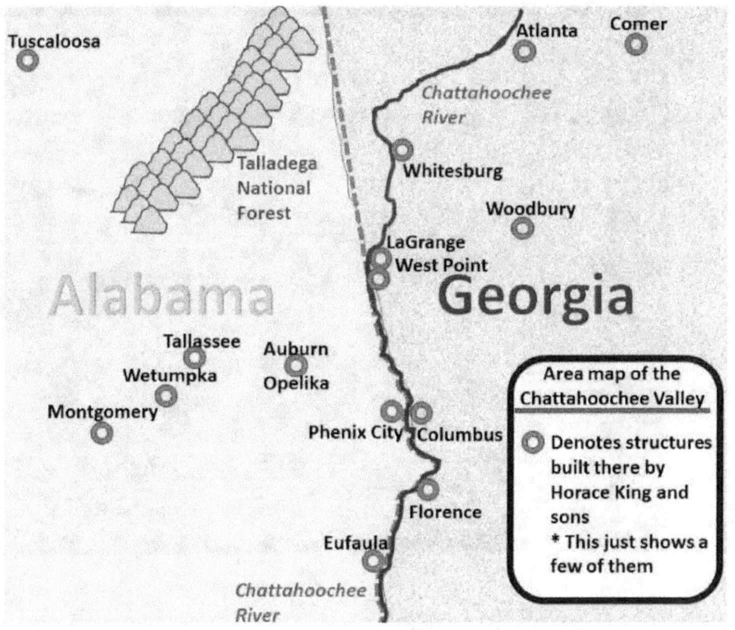

Horace King and sons' key bridges and structures of the Chattahoochee Valley
Author's Collection

Watson Mill Bridge (near Comer, Madison County, Georgia) from Survey HAER GA-140 Library of Congress, Prints & Photographs Division, Historic American Engineering Record of the Heritage Conservation and Recreation Service [HAER], Reproduction number [HAER GA-140]. (Today this bridge lies within the Watson Mill Bridge State Park, Madison County, Georgia).

*Interior view- Watson Mill Bridge.
HAER GA-140 Library of Congress, Prints &
Photographs Division*

In addition to bridges, Horace King also participated in construction or supervised the construction of numerous commercial buildings, warehouses, churches, homes and other noteworthy construction endeavors. For example, in 1869, King supervised the construction of the corn grist mill at "City Mills" in Columbus, Georgia.

City Mills Company, Eighteenth Street & First Avenue, Columbus, Muscogee County, Georgia. Photo from Survey HAER GA-25, Library of Congress, Prints & Photographs Division, Historic American Engineering Record of the Heritage Conservation and Recreation Service [HAER], Reproduction number [HAER GA-25].

In 1850, King constructed a pair of elegant three story floating (cantilevered) spiral staircases within the Alabama State Capitol building (Dexter Avenue, Montgomery, Montgomery County, Alabama). Photo: Library of Congress, Prints & Photographs Division, ALA,51-MONG,1-7. Historic American Buildings Survey, Library of Congress, Prints & Photographs Division.

Chapter 7

With the passage of time, the public has gained a greater appreciation for men and women of color whose histories were overlooked or nearly forgotten. King worked hard throughout his entire life and while he did suffer from the racial biases of that era, he rose above them through the construction of bridges by trade and deeds.

It is amazing that despite the passage of time and weather, many of King's masterful constructions are still in use today.

These architectural accomplishments bear witness to a genuinely skillful architect and engineer. Beginning in our bicentennial year of 1976 and continuing onward, King's legacy has achieved the prominence that his deeds so justly deserve.

His posthumous achievements and public recognition include:

Honors bestowed by the Museum of Arts and Sciences in Macon, Georgia as one of Georgia's "Notables: Imaginative Georgians and Their Discoveries", July 1, 1976; dedication of a Historical Marker at the corner of Broad and Dillingham Streets, Phenix City, Alabama, 1979; recognized by the State of Alabama for "Individual Outstanding Engineering or Technical Contributions and Accomplishments,

Tuscaloosa, Alabama, 1988; dedication of the "Horace King Bridge" (formerly 14th Street Bridge) and Historical Marker (by resolution of the Council of Columbus), Columbus, Georgia, 1988; dedication of the "Horace King Bridge" and Historical Marker placed in LaGrange, Georgia, 1989; induction into the State of Alabama Engineering Hall of Fame, Tuscaloosa, Alabama, 1989; dedication of "Horace King Park" at West Point Lake (seven miles west of LaGrange, Georgia); dedication of the "Horace King Street" Historical Marker in LaGrange, Georgia; Alabama State Capitol tribute to Horace King (Black History Month), Montgomery, Alabama, February 3, 2003; another historical marker honoring King is located in Cheraw, South Carolina where King and Godwin built their first bridge across the Pee Dee River.

Horace King listed (1868-1869 & 1870-1871) in the Alabama Historical Marker in Montgomery, Alabama

And finally, a remnant of the first bridge built by King can be seen on display in the Lyceum Museum, located at Town Green, Market Street in Cheraw, South Carolina.

In 2010, United States Representative Corrine Brown sponsored a Congressional Bill entitled, *Honoring and celebrating the contributions of African-Americans to the transportation and infrastructure of the United States.*

The bill's leading paragraph states, "Whereas African-Americans have played an instrumental role in developing and improving the transportation and infrastructure of the United States through leadership, design, and innovation."

Further into the narrative of the bill, Horace King is officially recognized with the following statement: "Whereas Horace King became known as "The Bridge Builder" for his work rebuilding bridges throughout Georgia, Mississippi, South Carolina, Alabama, New York, and many other States and passed on his legacy to his children through the family business, the Bridge Company." (24)

Horace King (1807-1885)
George Greene Collection

The life of Horace King exemplifies the power of the human spirit to overcome adversity. Although he was born into the tragic institution of slavery, he won his freedom and achieved impressive success.

Finally, like the bridges, he so proudly built, King's impressive works bear witness to the strength of the human heart and spirit. Horace King was certainly a remarkable man and his legacy remains visible to those who seek out his works.

End Notes (Sources)

1.   Letters and Recollections of Theodora Thomas. King Family File, Troup County Archives, LaGrange, Georgia; Horace King Files, George Greene Collection. Phenix City, Alabama.

2.   French, Thomas L. Jr. and Edward L. French. *Covered Bridges of Georgia*. Frenco Company: Columbus, Georgia, 1984.

3.   Records of the Office of City Clerk, Deed Book B, Contract for bridge between John Godwin and the City of Columbus, (Morris, Howell, & Morton to John Godwin). State of Georgia, County of Muscogee and City of Columbus, 17 July 1841.

4.   *The LaGrange Reporter*, LaGrange, Georgia. (October 13, 1871); Leonard, Tom. "Horace, The Bridge Builder King." Documentary Video, Auburn University Telecommunications/ ETV, Auburn University, Auburn, Alabama, 1996.

5.   Letters and Recollections of Theodora Thomas. King Family File, Troup County Archives, LaGrange, Georgia; Horace King Files, George Greene Collection. Phenix City, Alabama.

6.   Ibid.

7.   Cherry, F. L. <u>The History of Opelika and Agricultural Tributary Territory</u>. Genealogical Society of East Alabama, Inc. 1996, Pages 193-197.

8.   Alabama Legislative Acts: February 3, 1846, Number 292. Manumission of Horace King. Alabama Department of Archives and History. Montgomery, Alabama. Photo from the George Greene Collection.

9.   Cherry, F. L. <u>The History of Opelika and Agricultural Tributary Territory</u>. Genealogical Society of East Alabama, Inc. 1996, Pages 193-197.

10. Letters and Recollections of Theodora Thomas. King Family File, Troup County Archives, LaGrange, Georgia; Horace King Files, George Greene Collection. Phenix City, Alabama.

11. Cherry, F. L. <u>The History of Opelika and Agricultural Tributary Territory</u>. Genealogical Society of East Alabama, Inc. 1996, Pages 193-197.

12. The National Archives, Record Group Number 109.12, M374, Roll 16. Records of Confederate Soldiers from Alabama and Georgia.

13. The National Archives, Record Group Numbers 45 and 109.9, Records of the Confederate Navy (1861-1865). Records of the Naval Iron Works, Columbus, Georgia. Courtesy of the National Civil War Museum Archives.

14. Horace King to Robert Jemison Jr., Letter dated March 23, 1864. Jemison Papers. Tuscaloosa, Alabama, University of Alabama, (W. S. Hoole Special Collections Library). Also in George Greene Collection.

15. The National Archives, Record Group No. 233, Records of the U. S. House of Representatives Southern Claims Commission (1873-1878), Claim Number 19661 (Claim of Horace King).

16. Horace King Files, George Greene Collection. Phenix City, Alabama.

17. The National Archives, Record Group No. 233, Records of the U. S. House of Representatives Southern Claims Commission (1873-1878), Claim Number 19661 (Claim of Horace King).

18. Letters and Recollections of Theodora Thomas. King Family File, Troup County Archives, LaGrange, Georgia; Horace King Files, George Greene Collection. Phenix City, Alabama.

19. *The LaGrange Reporter*, LaGrange, Georgia, October 13, 1871.

20. Cherry, F. L. The History of Opelika and Agricultural Tributary Territory. Genealogical Society of East Alabama, Inc. 1996, Pages 193-197.

21.   *The LaGrange Reporter*, LaGrange, Georgia, June 4, 1887.

22. Red Oak Creek Bridge Historical Marker (Imlac, Georgia). Georgia State Department of Transportation.

23. French, Thomas L. Jr. and Edward L. French. *Covered Bridges of Georgia*. Frenco Company: Columbus, Georgia, 1984.

24. U.S. House of Representatives, Resolution 1085, *Honoring and celebrating the contributions of African-Americans to the transportation and infrastructure of the United States* Sponsor- Representative Corrine Brown, 111th U.S. Congressional House of Representatives, February 24, 2010.

Bibliography

Cherry, Rev. Francis. "History of Opelika..." 1883. Reprint, *Alabama Historical Quarterly* 14 (1953): 193-97.

Columbus Sun, (1850s-1880s) Columbus, Georgia.

Crogman, W.H. (William Henry) and H.F. Kletzing, *Progress of a race; From the Body of Slavery, Ignorance and Poverty to the Freedom of Citizenship, Intelligence, Affluence, Honor and Trust.* J.L. Nichols and Son. 1902..

Greene, Judge George Papers, 1950-2014, Greene Archives and Museum Collection. Russell County, Alabama.

Jemison, Robert Jr. Papers, 1797-1898, W. S. Hoole Special Collections Library, University of Alabama, Tuscaloosa, Alabama. This collection holds the only surviving correspondence of Horace King.

Lupold, John S. Collection (MC 197), Columbus State University Archives, Columbus, Georgia.

Lupold, John S., and Thomas L. French Jr. *Bridging Deep South Rivers: The Life and Legend of Horace King.* Athens: The University of Georgia Press, 2004.

Muscogee County, Georgia, Records of the Office of City Clerk, State of Georgia, County of Muscogee and City of Columbus.   64

The LaGrange Reporter, (1870s) LaGrange, Georgia.

Troup County Archives, Letters and Recollections of Theodora Thomas. King Family File, LaGrange, Georgia.

Weingardt, Richard G. (October 2007). *"Horace King: From Slave to Master Bridge Builder"*. Structure Magazine. National Council of Structural Engineers Associations.

List of Illustrations

	masters got the money unless the Negroes were freedmen). *George Greene Collection*
24	*Confederate Soldiers (A.M. Chandler and Silas Chandler, LC-DIG-ppmsca-40073), Library of Congress Prints and Photographs Division*
26	*1863 Confederate Navy receipt for Horace King contract work.* *George Greene Collection*
28	*C.S.S. Jackson (1864), USN Catalog #: NH 48026, United States Department of the Navy, US Naval Historical Center.*
29	*C.S.S. Jackson (1964), USN Catalog #: NH 45769, Georgia Historical Commission.* *U.S. Naval History and Heritage Command Photograph. Note: Although burned to the waterline and years later retrieved from the Chattahoochee River, the condition of the timbers is still solid. The ship's hull is on exhibit at the Confederate Naval Museum, Columbus, Georgia.*
36	*Battle of Columbus (April 16, 1865)* *Author's Collection*
37	*19th Century lithograph of Columbus, Georgia (excerpt depicting several King construction projects-mill, bridge and houses). George Greene Collection*
38	*African Americans voting for the first time during Reconstruction* *Library of Congress, Prints and Photographs Division*
39	*Alabama Reconstruction Legislature in front of the State House (1872).* *George Greene Collection*

40	*Ratified in 1870, the 15th Amendment of the US Constitution states, "The right of citizens...to vote shall not be denied or abridged...on account of race, color, or previous condition of servitude." Library of Congress, Prints and Photographs Division*
42	*Horace King and sons (circa 1869). Photos from W.H. Crogman's book entitled, Progress of a Race. George Greene Collection*
44	*Horace King in his final years. George Greene Collection*
47	*Red Oak Creek Bridge built by Horace King (Meriwether County, Georgia). Author's Collection*
49	*Map of the Chattahoochee Valley and Horace King and sons' structures Author's Collection*
50	*Watson Mill Bridge (near Comer, Madison County, Georgia) from Survey HAER GA-140 Library of Congress, Prints & Photographs Division, Historic American Engineering Record of the Heritage Conservation and Recreation Service [HAER], Reproduction number [HAER GA-140]. (Today this bridge lies within the Watson Mill Bridge State Park, Madison County, Georgia).*
51	*Interior view- Watson Mill Bridge. HAER GA-140 Library of Congress, Prints & Photographs Division*
52	*City Mills Company, Eighteenth Street & First Avenue, Columbus, Muscogee County, Georgia. Photo from Survey HAER*

	GA-25, Library of Congress, Prints & Photographs Division, Historic American Engineering Record of the Heritage Conservation and Recreation Service [HAER], Reproduction number [HAER GA-25].
53	*In 1850, King constructed a pair of elegant three story floating (cantilevered) spiral staircases within the Alabama State Capitol building (Dexter Avenue, Montgomery, Montgomery County, Alabama). Photo: Library of Congress, Prints & Photographs Division, ALA,51-MONG,1-7. Historic American Buildings Survey, Library of Congress, Prints & Photographs Division.*
56	*Horace King listed (1868-1869 & 1870-1871) in the Alabama Historical Marker in Montgomery, Alabama*
58	*Horace King (1807-1885)* *George Greene Collection*

Horace King – Timeline

1807 Horace is born in Cheraw, SC

1820- Ithiel Town patents Lattice Bridge

1827- Pee Dee River Bridge constructed

1832- Godwin and King move to
        Columbus, GA

1833- City Bridge built at Columbus

1838- Eufaula Bridge constructed

1839- West Point Bridge constructed
    - **April 28**- Horace and Frances
        married

1840- Red Oak Bridge constructed

1840-1846- Massive construction projects by Godwin and King (warehouses, courthouses, bridges, homes, churches

- **February 2**- Horace King emancipated by act of Alabama legislature

1855- Railroad bridge constructed at Columbus, GA

1858- Flint River bridge constructed at Albany, GA

1859, February 26- John Godwin died

1860, November 6- Abraham Lincoln elected as President of the USA

1861- The Civil War begins

1863- Horace King and sons begin
contract work for the Confederacy
at Columbus, GA
- **December**- Thomas Godwin
dies at Battle of Chattanooga

1864- CSS Jackson and CSS
Chattahoochee ironclads
constructed for the Confederacy

- Negro conscript bill passed by
CSA legislature- King requests
help from Robert Jemison

- **October**- Frances King died

1865- **April 9**- General Lee surrenders
the Confederacy to General
Grant in Virginia- war continues to
the west in GA and AL

April 16- Battle of Columbus, GA
and Girard, AL (Union burns
bridges)
- King family re-builds bridges and
Clapp's Factory

1868- Horace King won election to Alabama Legislature

1869- King family builds City Mills at Columbus

1870- Horace King re-elected to Alabama legislature

- King family builds Mobile & Girard railroad bridge at Columbus.
- 15th Amendment guarantees right to vote for all races

1872- Horace King steps down from Alabama legislature

- King family moves to LaGrange, GA

1879- Marshall King died

1885, May 27- Horace King died

Index

H
home	v,7,13
horses	8,34-35
hospital	26

I
ignorance	4,63
Indian	4,7,11-12,43
ironclad	27
Irwinton (Alabama- see Eufaula)	9

J
Jemison, Robert Jr.	18,30-31

K
King, Annie Elizabeth	12,41,45
King, Horace	(throughout)
King, Edmund	4,45
King, Frances	11-12,33,45
King, George	12,45
King, John	12,45
King, Marshall	12,45
King, Susan	4
King, Washington	12,45

X

Y

Z

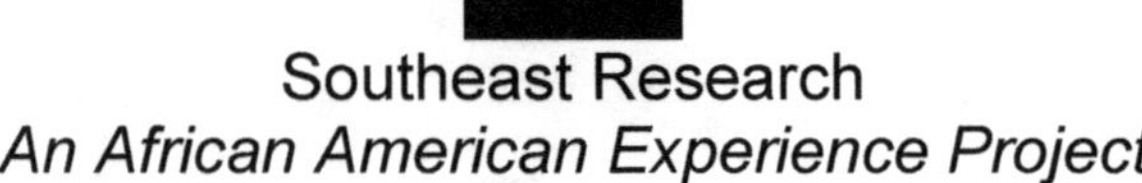

Southeast Research
An African American Experience Project

Southeast Research
An African American Experience Project

Southeast Research
An African American Experience Project